Original title:
The Poet's Garden

Copyright © 2025 Creative Arts Management OÜ
All rights reserved.

Author: Gideon Barrett
ISBN HARDBACK: 978-1-80566-642-4
ISBN PAPERBACK: 978-1-80566-927-2

Twilight Waltz of the Vivid Blooms

In the twilight, petals twirl,
Dancing round like a merry girl.
Bees with tiny top hats buzz,
Making music just because.

Laughter tickles the fragrant air,
As roses gossip without a care.
Tulips prance in bright array,
Winking at the ghost of day.

Remnants of a Verdant Past

In the thickets, a chair still stands,
Made of twigs and earthy bands.
A gnome snaps selfies with a squirrel,
Claiming he's the garden's pearl.

Old carrots laugh from the dirt,
Telling tales of juicy flirt.
Forget-me-nots with cheeky smiles,
Remember all the funny trials.

Enchantment in Each Leaf's Caress

Leaves are ticklish, soft and green,
Whispering secrets with a sheen.
A leaf sneezes, what a shock!
Tiny spiders wearing socks!

Vines twist like they're doing yoga,
Chasing dreams of a sweet aroma.
Petal-dressers prance along,
Each one ready for a song.

Musing on the Tangy Fruits

Fruits giggle on their sunny beds,
With little hats atop their heads.
Oranges bounce, lemons roll,
A fruity game that takes a toll.

"Hey there, berry!" the melon sings,
"Let's flip-flop, oh, the joy it brings!"
Grapes crack jokes until they burst,
In this place, laughter is the first.

Scale of the Morning Glories

In a riot of colors, they twist and twine,
Morning glories giggle, sipping sunshine.
They bloom with a splash, a vernal parade,
But whisper to bees, 'This nectar's home-made!'

Each petal a dancer, with pollen as prize,
They flirt with the breeze, while bees roll their eyes.
'Why are you late?' the sunflower shouts,
'With these morning delights, you're missing the bout!'

Nature's Scrolls of Confessions

The trees hold secrets, they giggle and sway,
With roots deep in gossip, they bark out the play.
'I saw you last night!' the old oak declares,
While the lilacs blush, hiding all of their flares.

Flowers whisper softly, with petals aflutter,
'Did you hear what the tulips did under the gutter?'
Nature's scrolls flutter with tales to be told,
As vines weave a story of mischief and bold.

Radiance of the Opening Flower

With a yawn and a stretch, the petals unfold,
A quirky performance, never quite old.
'Is it morning,' it asks, 'or am I just late?'
The sun chuckles back, 'Just don't be irate!'

As it blossoms in hues, a riotous cheer,
'Buzz off!' says the bumblebee, 'I'm trying to steer!'
Each bloom is a weirdo, a character rare,
In this garden of antics, joy's floating in air.

Cursive Lines on the Garden Wall

Roses doodle whispers on rough brick and stone,
Sneaking words to the moon, who'll never atone.
'How are you?' they giggle, with thorns on their sides,
'We're blooming divas, with nothing to hide!'

Vines scribble love notes, tangled in flair,
'You're thorny but charming, let's dance if you dare!'
The fresh ink of petals expands with a laugh,
In this garden of secrets, let's craft a new path.

Blooming Words in Soft Twilight

In evening's glow, the daisies chat,
Discussing gossip, who's slim and fat.
The tulips giggle, oh what a sight,
While marigolds joke, stretching left and right.

Bees join the fun, buzzing quite loud,
Wearing tiny hats, they're feeling proud.
With pollen jokes that never get old,
Each bloom's a comedian, brave and bold.

Secrets of the Dappled Grove

In the grove where shadows dance and play,
Squirrels debate on the best nut buffet.
A chatty robin sings in twirls and hops,
While wise old owls are gossiping flops.

"Did you see that mushroom? Such a sight!"
The daisies whisper, "Who's wrong or right?"
Rhymes sprout freely like weeds in the sun,
As laughter and secrets become one.

Rhythms of the Blossom

Petals sway to the rhythm of breeze,
Frogs wear sunglasses, lounging with ease.
Crickets tap dance on a lily pad,
While flowers giggle, never looking sad.

"Did you hear that joke about the bee?"
It buzzed in, best punchline, oh so free.
With each fragrant laugh that fills the air,
Nature's comedy waits everywhere.

Stanzas in the Shade

Under trees where branches lean and twist,
Laughter emerges like morning mist.
The shadows join in a quirky parade,
A symphony of chuckles in the shade.

A daffodil dreams of a stand-up show,
While the breeze sweeps in to steal the flow.
Nature's own antics create such delight,
A curated gallery of funny sight.

Ties of the Weeping Willow

Beneath the willow's veil so grand,
Laughter echoes, hand in hand.
We pretend we're trees, standing tall,
Trying not to burst into a brawl.

The squirrels giggle, high in their nests,
While branches sway, in funny quests.
We tie knots in laughter, what a sight,
As leaves fall down, a comical flight.

The Scribe of Green Thumbs

With fingertips dusted, soil in a heap,
I scribble my tales where daisies sleep.
The zucchini whispers a joke to the beans,
While carrots chuckle in neat, straight lines.

Each plant has a story, you just have to ask,
Like how the chives wear a sneaky mask.
They think they're funny, with their little green hats,
While the onions cry, amidst all the chats.

Fragments of Fragrance in Still Air

In a world where scents take the lead,
The roses tease, "We're what you need!"
Lavender leans in, with a wink so sly,
"Sniff us well, but don't you cry!"

The daffodils giggle, a bright yellow crew,
They dance in the breeze like they're in a zoo.
"Come smell our stories," they proudly declare,
"Just watch out for bees; they don't play fair!"

Diaries of Drenched Petals

In puddles of rain, petals lay bare,
Writing their stories with delicate flair.
"Today we splashed, oh what a delight!
We twirled in the droplets, what a fun sight!"

With a tap dance of water, they giggle with cheer,
Sharing their secrets, it's so clear.
"Tomorrow we'll bloom, but today we just play,
Drenched and delighted, let's save the day!"

Awakening the Silent Buds

In a quiet nook where daisies droop,
A gnome does dance with a rubber scoop.
He shouts to blooms, so shy and small,
"Get up, you lazy petals, stand tall!"

A daffodil giggles, a tulip grins,
While sneaky snails play hide and sins.
They plot mischief, oh what a scene,
As sunlight breaks through, all fresh and keen.

The Color of Thoughtful Breezes

Whispers of wind tease the tiny seed,
"Dress up in colors, that's what you need!"
They twirl around, in vibrant delight,
Creating a rainbow that took flight.

Petunias snicker, colors galore,
As pansies perform, wanting an encore.
The breeze mocks the rose with a cheeky laugh,
"Without your thorns, you'd be a craft!"

Metaphors of the Moonlit Vines

In the night's embrace, with stars so wide,
Grapevines gossip as the owls glide.
"We're spiraled poets, tangled in rhyme,
Our words twist like tendrils, all in prime!"

A lizard winks from the woven tight,
"Metaphors hug me, it feels just right!"
They dream of juice in a glass so fine,
"Sipped under the moon, let's birth a vine!"

Four Seasons of Unspoken Lines

Winter's whispers come, oh so slow,
While squirrels argue, they steal the show.
"A nut for you and a nut for me,
Let's trade our secrets — what could they be?"

Spring giggles bright, with blossoms in tow,
As tulips say, "Let's make a row!"
They bicker and bloom, with colors to cheer,
Each petal a secret, all bright and clear.

Summer sings sweet, the laughter grows,
With bees busy buzzing, as if there are prose.
"Dance with the sun, let shadows entwine,
We are the chums of the bright sunshine!"

Autumn arrives with a rustling sound,
Falling leaves sprinkle, a colorful crown.
"Let's chat of harvest, the fruit of our toil,
In whispers of pumpkins, pickled and foil!"

Serenity in Each Stem

In the garden, socks with holes,
Dance with daisies, play the roles.
Worms wear hats and sing a song,
While beetles strut, they can't go wrong.

Rabbits laugh at the sun's bright rays,
As they munch through the grass in plays.
Crickets call with a rhythmic beat,
Celebrating both bugs and feet.

When tulips giggle, blooms in cheer,
We'd tip our hats, but they'd just leer.
In this patch, where chaos reigns,
Life's quirks sprout from stubborn grains.

Verses in Vines

In twisted tendrils, legends grow,
Where grapes recite their tales in tow.
With rhymes that bounce like bouncing balls,
And ivy climbing up the walls.

Lemons joke and tell a pun,
While peppers duel under the sun.
A corn stalk breaks into a dance,
And lettuce sways in a leafy trance.

When carrots wear shoes that squeak,
Tomatoes burst out with a cheeky peek.
With laughter sprouting in every row,
There's no place funnier, this we know!

Requiem for the Withering Leaf

A leaf fell down with a funny frown,
It whispered tales of green renown.
"Help, I'm shriveling, please don't stare!"
But the breeze just giggled, without a care.

Caterpillars snickered, "What a show!"
As the leaf confessed it didn't want to go.
Bees buzzed jokes to cheer it up,
While ants marched by with a tiny cup.

One last laugh as it spiraled away,
With a twirl and a spin, it chose to play.
In the soil, it planted a wish to thrive,
And became the best joke of spring alive!

Flourishing in Folio

In a book of blooms, pages turn,
Where daisies learn what daisies yearn.
A plot with petals weaving tales,
And laughter sprouting on the trails.

Ferns wearing glasses read aloud,
While sunflowers prance and feel so proud.
The daisies giggle, gossiping bright,
Sharing secrets late into the night.

Roses sigh, wearing their thorns,
"Life's too short for worn-out warns!"
Petunias brew a tea of cheer,
While pansies paint smiles, far and near.

Traces of Dreams in the Climbing Vines

In a maze of twirls, my thoughts take flight,
A squirrel named Gary stole my pen last night.
He scribbles on leaves, quite a crafty guy,
His art? A nutty masterpiece, oh my!

The petals giggle, caught in a breeze,
As I chase my hat, tangled in the trees.
A ladybug laughs, spinning in a swirl,
She's the queen of this jungle, my little pearl!

The daisies hold secrets in chatter so bright,
"What's that you're wearing?" with delight and fright.
"Haha!" I reply, "Just my socks on my ears!"
They titter and wiggle, washing away fears.

So come join the fun in this whimsical glade,
Where dreams intertwine and laughter won't fade.
The chirps and the giggles create a fine art,
In the embrace of the vines, we'll never part.

Scribbles of the Hummingbird's Dance

In bright little flutters, the dancers appear,
With wings like confetti, they bring joy near.
They sip on the sweetness, a nectar parade,
While I trip on a root, my balance betrayed.

A bumblebee buzzes, "Hey friend, let's play!"
But I'm stuck in the mud, oh what a day!
With wildflower giggles, they cheer and they tease,
As I wriggle and wiggle, releasing a wheeze.

The clouds chuckle softly, their billowy spray,
As I join in the dance, come what may.
A caterpillar grins, twirling with ease,
"I may be slow, but I'm ready to seize!"

Through chuckles and sparkles, the breezes do weave,
A tapestry bright, oh how we believe!
In this playful spectacle, joy knows no bounds,
Every giggle and grin in nature resounds.

Strokes of Sunshine on Crimson Blooms

Beneath the sun, the flowers dance,
Their petals bright in wild romance.
A bee slips by with antics grand,
While butterflies plot a prank on land.

The wind just giggles, sways the trees,
It tickles blooms with playful ease.
A daisy wears a silly hat,
While roses gossip—oh, how they're brat!

Each morning brings a cheeky grin,
As weeds jump in for the win.
The garden is a playful place,
Where flora flaunts its funny face.

In every corner, laughter grows,
As daisies peek where no one knows.
And with each twist of nature's mix,
It crafts a scene of joyful tricks.

Interludes of the Thirsting Garden

A brook trips over stones and laughs,
While thirsty plants do silly halves.
With every drop, they shimmy and shake,
Performing shows for laughter's sake.

Sunlight spills like golden syrup,
On leafy greens that start to stir up.
With roots that wriggle, worms parade,
In this botanical escapade.

Petunias dream of grand ballet,
While daisies joke, 'It's our big day!'
But gardener's hose, in jetting spree,
Drenches all in playful glee.

The cactus winks, quite prickly though,
Hiding puns in every row.
Thus, nature joins in merry fights,
In interludes of pure delights.

The Hidden Scripts of Nature's Artistry

Among the leaves, a story brews,
Of hidden scripts in quiet hues.
The earth laughs softly, dirt on cheek,
With secrets whispered, never meek.

Squirrels giggle, tossing acorns,
While ants march on, with tiny horns.
A tulip dons a cloak of stripes,
Pretending it's part of the circus types.

Each shadow tells a jester's tale,
Of hopping frogs and playful snails.
They plot and scheme beneath the trees,
In hidden scripts that play with ease.

Nature's canvas, wild and bright,
Crafts giggles in the morning light.
With every breeze, the stories shift,
In laughter's dance, the flowers gift.

Tidal Waves of Scented Memories

The lilacs giggle with scented grace,
As honeyed breezes fill the space.
Daisies shout, "We smell divine!"
While violets pout, "But look at mine!"

Each bloom recalls a silly jest,
Whispered between their fragrant quests.
Marigolds chuckle, side by side,
No secrets kept, they just can't hide.

The night blooms giggle in the dark,
With fireflies joining in their spark.
Each petal's scent is a memory,
Swirling tales of pure comedy.

As waves of fragrance ebb and flow,
The garden's laughter starts to grow.
In every whiff, joy intertwines,
With scented memories of funny times.

Musing by Moonlight

Under the glow of a giant cheese,
I scribble my thoughts, hoping to please.
The daisies giggle, the roses shade,
While tulips dance, all unafraid.

A squirrel with swagger steals my pen,
Claiming the title of 'best writer' again.
I try to catch him; he ducks with grace,
Reminding me that I'm way out of place.

The moon winks down, it knows our game,
With laughter and laughter, we share no shame.
Each word I write bounces with glee,
In this garden of mischief, we all agree!

A frog croaks jokes from his lily pad chair,
His punchlines bloom like flowers in air.
As I pen my verses in the night's embrace,
The moon giggles lightly at this silly chase.

Ink-Pool Reflections

In puddles of ink beneath the trees,
I see my thoughts reflected with ease.
A ladybug jots down a quirky rhyme,
While crickets chirp, keeping perfect time.

The water's a stage, and I'm the star,
As goldfish laugh from their glassy bazaar.
Writing in ripples, my pen takes flight,
In this ink-pool, everything feels right.

A butterfly flutters, keen on my quill,
Oh, the cheek! Thinking it's here for the thrill.
We sketch funny tales with each little splash,
As giggles abound in this poetic bash.

The reflections chuckle, they know we're wise,
In this whimsical plot, no one's a surprise.
And as I scribble, the sun starts to snooze,
I dip my pen deep for more silly blues!

Symphony of Sprouts

In the corner, the spinach starts to dance,
A waltz with the carrots; oh, what a chance!
Radishes giggle; they roll in delight,
While peas join the party, all dressed in bright.

The tomatoes boast with their plump little cheeks,
Sharing tall tales for the bold and the meek.
But lettuce whispers, 'I'm feeling shy',
As the turnips tease, 'You're just a salad pie!'

The cabbage croons out a melodic tune,
Echoed by flowers beneath the moon.
With roots tapping softly on the cool ground,
They create a symphony that's truly profound.

As nature claps and the crickets encore,
We dance with our sprouts till we can't take more.
In this garden of giggles, no moment is grim,
For each leafy note makes the laughter brim.

Palette of Seasons

Spring arrives in polka-dot boots,
Painting the daisies and charming the roots.
While summer throws parties with sunshine rays,
As bees buzz in dresses, they're ready to play.

Autumn comes waltzing, with leaves in a whirl,
Claiming the pumpkin as nature's own pearl.
Scarecrows laugh loudly; they finagle a deal,
With crows hoping for that last meal's appeal.

Winter rolls in, with a snowy white cape,
Building snowmen who pose and escape.
They chuckle and frolic, with carrots for noses,
While snowflakes giggle on soft, frosty roses.

Each season a color, a canvas anew,
Blending in laughter, in every hue.
As I paint my thoughts on this vibrant spree,
The garden transforms into a wild jubilee!

Whispers Among the Petals

In the patch of bright daisies,
A bee wore a hat quite crazy.
He buzzed with such flair,
Like he had no care.

A sunflower cracked jokes so sunny,
Telling tales of big, fat money.
But the roses rolled eyes,
As they plotted their cries.

The wind joined the fun with a bow,
Tickling leaves, saying, "Take a vow!"
That laughter should grow,
Like fruits in a row.

And under the moon's playful gaze,
The garden danced in silly ways.
With vine-tangled cheer,
Joy bloomed everywhere.

Verses in Bloom

In this patch of bright flair,
A daffodil took to the air.
He wore a bowtie, so neat,
Claiming he's hard to beat.

The tulips held a tea spree,
Where daisies danced with glee.
Their jokes were quite wild,
As nature beamed like a child.

The carrots debated with pride,
On whose green tops would reside.
"Mine are much taller, so there!"
They clashed with a garden flare.

With every petal's delightful quirk,
The blooms knew how to work.
In this garden of laughs,
They shared joyful gaffs.

Echoes of Lavender Dreams

The lavender swayed with delight,
Making scents that felt just right.
It whispered of dreams so absurd,
Like a snail playing in a bird.

A shy thyme decided to sing,
Its voice was like a kazoo's ring.
Even the basil joined in,
With a dance that was all in spin.

The chives were a cheeky bunch,
Holding contests for the world's crunch.
With each snip and snarl,
Their humor had a pearl.

And as night wrapped the flowers tight,
They chuckled beneath the starlight.
In a garden of giggles,
Their joy softly wiggles.

Stanzas Beneath the Willow

Beneath a willow, snug and wide,
A rabbit practiced its pride.
With a top hat and cane,
It danced in the rain.

Grasshoppers tapped their tiny shoes,
Grouping to share their good news.
They joked about flies,
Under the big blue skies.

The flowers giggled, swayed in sync,
Planning pranks on the big pink stink.
"Oh dear, what a sight!"
They laughed with delight.

And as dusk lit the garden's floor,
A chorus rang out, a fun uproar.
In shadows so meek,
Joy colored the peek.

The Sonnet of Sunflowers

In a field of gold, they dance and sway,
With heads so high, they greet the day.
They gossip with bees in a buzzing buzz,
And laugh at the clouds, as only they does.

Their seeds are a treasure for birds that dine,
Yet some think they're hats – but hats aren't divine!
They stand so proud, like a cheeky bunch,
Waving at passersby, seeking a crunchy lunch.

Shadows of the Singing Trees

The trees are crooners with arms stretched wide,
Swaying to rhythms that they can't hide.
They whisper to squirrels, with humor untold,
Of acorns and acappella, the antics unfold.

The leaves are their fans, they flutter and cheer,
While branches tap dance, oh dear, oh dear!
Their roots tell tales of a wobbly past,
Of lightning strikes bold and shadows cast.

Blossoms of Ink and Imagination

In the artist's mind, flowers bloom bright,
With petals of paper, ink spills in flight.
Each stroke a giggle, each color a tease,
They bloom in odd shapes, like a puzzling breeze.

Paintbrushes waltz, as the canvas sways,
And thoughts turn to blooms in whimsical ways.
The roses with pens write poems so spry,
While daisies play tricks on the butterflies.

Ode to the Dandelion

A puffball of joy in the sun's warm light,
You spread your seeds, like thoughts taking flight.
With a wink to the kids who blow with delight,
You conquer the yard, with your daring fight.

You wear a crown made of sunshine and cheer,
A weed, or a flower? Let's make it clear!
For every time someone snubs your bright face,
You laugh and keep growing, a true spunky grace.

Lyrical Blooms in Every Color

In patches bright with vibes so playful,
A daffodil joked with a rose so graceful.
The tulips danced, a frolicsome sight,
While daisies laughed till day turned to night.

Sunflowers shrugged with a cheeky grin,
Complaining of bees that buzzed under skin.
A raven perched, with a frown on its face,
Declared the blooms had won the race!

With colors that sparkled like quirky dreams,
Petunias giggled at their leafy schemes.
In this wild patch, both silliness reigned,
A riot of hues, where laughter maintained.

So prance with joy in vibrant delight,
For flowers know humor, and they bloom bright.
With nature's quirks as sharp as a quill,
Each bloom whispers secrets, a funny thrill.

Tending to the Winter's Remnants

With snowflakes gone, the garden's awoken,
A patch of mud, oh what a token!
The worms are giggling, wiggling playfully,
While frostbitten leaves argue disgracefully.

A rake seems shy, tucked under a bush,
It dreams of spring in a triumphant hush.
The snips and shears chatter in delight,
As they plot to trim with all of their might.

Yet weeds pop up like jokes on a stage,
Pulling pranks, they're all the rage!
A dandelion whispers, 'Here I remain,'
While gardeners groan, oh what a strain!

In this wild cleanup, laughter prevails,
As winter's remnants tell funny tales.
For in every plant's clumsy return,
There's joy in the chaos, hearts brightly burn.

Petal-Crowned Reflections

With petals placed on heads like crowns,
The bees debate who wears the gowns.
Dandelions strut with a golden flair,
While garden gnomes giggle, caught unaware.

Raindrops chuckle, tickling the rose,
As the daisies giggle with their sunlit prose.
Reflecting on life, with clumsy finesse,
In the mirror of ponds, they deem it a mess.

Beetles buzz like tiny old champs,
As mint leaves sip from their tiny lamps.
They dream of the day they'd win floral lore,
In this raucous banquet of petals galore.

So crown each bloom with laughter and cheer,
For nature's own humor is ever so near.
In joy and in blooms of colors amassed,
Petal-crowned jesters, forever steadfast.

Chasing Shadows in Green Corners

In shady nooks where sunbeams hide,
The garden critters take joy in their ride.
A squirrel does flips, proclaiming its flair,
While butterflies whisper they just don't care.

A shadow leaps, and the lilies all squeal,
Chasing the sunlight, spinning a wheel.
The turf rolls over with giggles and grins,
While nature's own jester absorbs all the sins.

Grasshoppers spring like jesters in flight,
Skipping on raindrops with reckless delight.
Fern fronds wave, a delicate jest,
Trying their best to laugh at the rest.

So gather the giggles from green corners wide,
Chasing the shadows with whimsy as guide.
In this leafy cocoon where antics are rife,
Laughter blooms freely, with joy as its life.

Flourishing Phrases

In a plot where words take root,
The daisies giggle in their boots.
They dance around with rhyming joy,
While worms compose their verses coy.

Bees buzz in lines, a buzzing choir,
As ants recite their little choir.
With laughter sewn in every seam,
They sprout up dreams and sticky cream.

Sunflowers wear their crowns so bright,
Chasing clouds with all their might.
While tulips wink and tease and twirl,
In this happy sunlit swirl.

So gather 'round, you bards and sows,
In this plot where nonsense grows.
For every sprout holds tales to share,
Of puns and giggles filling air.

Songs of the Silent Sprout

In silence sits a timid sprout,
With thoughts too big to let them out.
It dreams of singing loud and clear,
While dodging all the garden's fear.

A raindrop falls, it starts to hum,
Vibrations dance, it's quite the drum.
As insects clap with tiny hands,
The sprout forms bands with leafy strands.

At night, the stars all wink and glow,
Encouraging the sprout to flow.
It belts out tunes to moonlit skies,
With melodies that spark surprise.

Yet in the morning, down it goes,
For garden life has many woes.
But wait! It sprouts back up, you see,
With songs of joy, so wild and free.

Whispers Among the Petals

Petals gossip in colors bright,
Sharing secrets in morning light.
A rose confesses to the vine,
While daisies play a game of twine.

Sunlight tickles the shyest bloom,
As bees come buzzing close to zoom.
They trade ideas on how to sway,
And giggle at the bumblebee ballet.

Each flower dreams of hats and shoes,
While nurturing their playful views.
With witty barbs, they jest and spar,
A garden realm, a funny bazaar.

Yet when the gusty winds appear,
They hold on tight, suppress a cheer.
For in this dance of sway and bend,
Their laughter echoes without end.

Verses Beneath the Willow

Beneath the willow, whispers creep,
Where tangled roots and secrets seep.
The frogs compose a nightly play,
While crickets chirp the night away.

With shadows cast, the fireflies blink,
Plotting tales over leaf and ink.
They mix a potion, a rhyme or two,
While giggling low, just me and you.

A squirrel jests from branch to branch,
In acorn hats, they've got quite the chance.
With jumps and flips, they write their lore,
Creating mischief, always wanting more.

As moonlight weaves through leaves so fine,
The willow smiles with a cheeky line.
In laughter shared, all troubles cease,
A garden of verses, a sweet release.

Echoing Gardens

In a patch of weeds, we find a snack,
A strawberry thief dashed with a quack.
The daisies giggle, swaying in chat,
While bunnies debate who's fatter than fat.

The sunflowers bow, give a sun-salute,
But bees steal the spotlight, how rude, how cute!
A turtle wearing glasses, oh what a sight,
Jokes with a snail on a lazy light night.

A friendly breeze whispers through the grass,
Spinach plants shuffle, as if they could pass.
"I'm super fresh!" claims the cucumber green,
While carrots just sigh, "We're rarely seen."

In this world of blooms, laughter unfolds,
Where plants, like children, are bold and uncontrolled.
Each petal a giggle, each leaf a cheer,
In the garden of jest, there's nothing to fear.

Petal-Paved Pathways

A path of petals leads us astray,
With roses that wriggle, they dance and sway.
An insect parade, with pizzazz so grand,
Could start a conga—imagine the band!

The tulips are twirling, a swirling spree,
While lilies gossip, "Who's cuter than we?"
Chattering daisies gossip and tease,
As garden gnomes wave, "Just do as you please!"

The hedge has a secret, it whispers and laughs,
Holding tales of bumblebees' comical gaffs.
Each footfall creates a confetti of dreams,
Floral adventures are never as they seem.

Here, fruit and flowers play silly games,
A fruit fly named Bob, with wildly strange aims.
"Let's juggle some cherries!" he dares with a grin,
And laughter erupts as the show must begin.

Versing the Verdant

In leafy lanes where chuckles abound,
The broccoli's rapping, a veggie sound.
A garlic bulb breaks into a song,
"Lettuce unite, we can't be wrong!"

Pansies wear glasses, pretentious, yet bright,
While thyme throws a party that lasts through the night.
Cucumbers roll in, with picnic supplies,
"Let's snack on the sun, under these blue skies!"

The weeds tell tall tales of heroic fights,
With dandelions bragging of their heights.
The lilacs snicker, "We smell so divine,
While those pesky old weeds just wish they were mine!"

In this green paradise, where humor grows free,
Each verse blossoms, so grand and carefree.
So raise up a toast, with blossoms clinking,
To the wildness of whimsy, forever winking!

Lament of the Last Leaf

One leaf hangs on, but who's keeping track?
He sighs with a shiver, a real heart attack.
The wind whispers softly, "Time to depart,"
Yet he's got a joke, a literal work of art.

"I'm not falling down, I'm practicing flight!"
He quips to the branch, chuckling with delight.
The acorns applaud, though they're barely awake,
As the last leaf giggles, "For goodness' sake!"

The seasons parade, and all seem to cheer,
Past blossoms and blooms, no worry or fear.
In the grapevines, spirits soar as they craze,
While the last leaf embraces his final hooray.

So here's to the moments, both silly and sly,
In gardens of laughter, where leaves learn to fly.
With humor our compass, we'll dance through the night,
For life's just a riot—so let's get it right!

Songs of the Blooming Season

In a patch of daisies, sit a bee,
Buzzing tunes as sweet as can be.
The lilies giggle, the violets sway,
While tulips dance the night away.

The sunflowers grin with a golden cheer,
As squirrels debate which nut to steer.
A butterfly sneezes, lands with a thud,
And shakes off confetti from last night's flood.

The roses blush, oh what a sight,
A prank from a breeze that gave them a fright.
They whisper secrets to pansies around,
While frogs croon symphonies, oh what a sound!

So here in the blooms, laughter's the goal,
With every petal, there's joy in the soul.
The season's a party, let's all take a chance,
In this colorful realm, we all love to dance.

Footprints Among the Flora

Stomping through meadows, oh what a mess,
A gopher declares, "Oh, what a dress!"
Mushrooms giggle as they trip on a vine,
While wallflowers sigh, "This garden's divine."

A hedgehog in slippers is chasing a beetle,
They wiggle and jiggle, it's such a fun riddle.
A squirrel in shades holds a nutty parade,
Throwing acorns like confetti, oh what a cascade!

Petunias whisper to dandelions, too,
"Can you believe the nonsense we do?"
Flip-flops are trailing in a sea of lush green,
With footprints like cookies, a slapstick routine.

From daisies to clovers, laughter takes flight,
As crayons of colors emerge in the light.
In the soil of giggles, together we roam,
These whimsical blooms feel just like home.

Gossamer Threads of Inspiration

A spider is busy, weaving his dreams,
With threads that shimmer like moonlit beams.
The grasshoppers chirp with a fumble and buzz,
While ants march in line, they're always a fuss.

A jay steals a berry, oh what a spree,
He hops on a branch, singing joyfully.
The violets applaud in their soft, lilac hue,
While garlic chives gossip about love's debut.

A tall sunflower's practicing her pose,
As she cracks jokes with her friend, the rose.
The daisies are rivals in a contest of cheer,
While tulips compete for the best fashion year.

In this realm of the quirky, the funny takes charge,
With every bright blossom, we revel and enlarge.
Let's laugh and create, let our feelings ignite,
In this theater of nature, everything's right.

Fables from the Floral Abyss

In the depths of the garden where stories reside,
A gnarled old oak shares wisdom with pride.
"Beware of the gnome with a penchant for pranks,"
He painted the flowers in bizarre, wild ranks.

The tulips debated who wore the best hue,
While begonias cackled, "We're winning, who knew?"
A daffodil giggles, and slips on a bee,
Landing right square on a branch of a tree.

With whispers of tales from roots underground,
The worms tell of treasures that nobody found.
By the lily-pad pond, laughter fills air,
As frogs put on plays, who needs Broadway flair?

So join in the fun, let's share in this jest,
With every new bloom, we'll make memories best.
In this patch of delight, where wild stories roam,
Friendships grow deeper, in this whimsical home.

In the Heart of Blossoms

In the heart of blooms so bright,
A bumblebee gave quite a fright.
He buzzed and tumbled, oh what fun,
As petals danced beneath the sun.

Lettuce hats on every head,
Radishes turned bright, instead.
In colors bold they pranced about,
With laughter ringing, there's no doubt.

The daisies flipped their petals wide,
While violets giggled, full of pride.
Bees played tag on floral swings,
In this circus of living things.

Oh, but sneaky weeds would creep,
In this garden, nothing's cheap.
They tried to join the flower ball,
But all they did was watch and sprawl.

Revelations from the Edible Patch

In a patch where veggies talk,
Tomatoes strut and make a mock.
They wear their skins of crimson hue,
And boast about their salad crew.

Cucumbers in a race so sly,
Roll over radishes, oh my!
With every twist and every turn,
The carrots watch, their envy burns.

Potatoes tried to jump and glide,
But tripped and tumbled, oh what pride!
Their skins were muddy, but they swore,
They'd practice dancing, and then soar.

A garlic bulb, with clove so bold,
Declared it's worth its weight in gold.
Yet every veggie held its breath,
So worried they might end in chef's!

Voyages Through the Verdant

In a jungle of leafy greens,
A squirrel plotted funny schemes.
He built a raft of twigs and leaves,
To sail the stream where laughter weaves.

Onboard he had a band of ants,
In tiny hats, they took their stance.
With acorns for their drum and flute,
They rocked the waves, oh how they scoot!

A frog, with pep on lily pads,
Joined in the fun, dismissing fads.
He croaked a tune, the squirrels danced,
In this adventure, all entranced.

But suddenly, a wind so bold,
Sent hats and ants into the cold.
Yet giggles echoed through the trees,
As they regrouped with squeaky wheeze.

Bloodroot Dances in the Breeze

In shadows where the bloodroots play,
They twirl and spin the night away.
With stems like little party hats,
They shuffle close, avoiding chats.

A moth boogies close to the ground,
While crickets make their joyful sound.
The moonlight spills on leafy greens,
Transforming dark to dance routines.

The owls hoot out the disco beats,
While foxes tap with tiny feet.
Insects buzz on a sugar high,
As petals wave all night to fly.

But dawn approaches, night must close,
The flowers yawn, the moment chose.
Yet still they dream of such a tease,
As day breaks soft through rustling leaves.

Fables Whispers Between the Rows

In the patch where stories roam,
Tomatoes giggle, they call it home.
A radish wore a tiny hat,
While carrots danced, imagine that!

The beans all whispered tales of flight,
How squashes tread the moonlit night.
A cabbage tried to tell a joke,
But ended up a leafy cloak!

Underneath the broccoli trees,
A spinach sat with just a breeze.
It fondly spoke of jelly beans,
And roamed the land of baked potato scenes.

So gather, friend, let laughter sway,
In this garden of whimsy, let's sing and play.
For in each row, a fable grows,
A merry mix of highs and lows.

Crawling Through the Fern's Embrace

A snail with shades moved slow and proud,
Declaring, 'I'm the coolest, loud.'
Beside him, crickets formed a band,
While worms kept rhythm, oh so grand!

The ferns swayed gently, having fun,
They whispered secrets, one by one.
A lizard joined with a flick and grin,
Telling tales of where he's been.

But watch out! A frog jumped high,
And landed near a startled pie.
"Oh, don't mind me," it said with flair,
"Just practicing my leaps, beware!"

So here among the ferns, we see,
Life's a party, wild and free.
With laughter shared through bugs and leaves,
In this embrace, the spirit weaves.

Shadows of the Wandering Butterfly

A butterfly flits with lessons learned,
Dancing shadows while pollen turned.
It bumped a flower, sweet surprise,
A daisy laughed, "You've got no ties!"

Through blooming paths, the colors clash,
Where tulips prance and peonies flash.
With every turn, a giggle bursts,
As bees do cartwheels, oh, how they thirst!

The sun above, a witty jester,
Tells flowers, "You're the finest dresser!"
While clouds chuckle, soft and puffy,
Encouraging blooms to feel all fluffy.

So dance, dear wings, don't look down,
In fields of laughter, wear your crown.
For in each shadow that you glide,
Lies a world of joy and pride.

Gleanings from the Scented Shrubs

Among the shrubs, the scents arise,
A rosemary bush wore a disguise.
"I'm sage," it claimed with aromatic grace,
While lavender blushed, a smiling face!

The thyme had tales of spice and cheer,
Whispering secrets for all to hear.
"Chili's got moves, it's quite a ball,
But watch it dance, it'll make you sprawl!"

One spice got lost, confused and meek,
"Oh dear, am I parsley or a freak?"
The mint chimed in with a cooling smile,
"Just hop aboard; let's groove a while!"

So gather, herbs, let's spice the day,
In hills of flavor, come out and play.
For in their shrubby, scented spaces,
Lies a banquet of friendly faces.

The Language of Leaves

In whispers soft, the leaves confide,
They gossip kindly, while swaying wide.
"Did you hear about the rose's flair?"
"Oh please, she's just a show-off, I swear!"

The oak chuckles, with chestnut glee,
"The daisies think they're quite the spree.
But do they know? The weeds are sly,
They plot and plan, oh my, oh my!"

Each twig a jester, each branch a clown,
Drawing smiles in this leafy town.
While petals blush in vibrant hues,
They laugh at the gardener's overdues!

So come and listen, the trees will tease,
In this green expanse where laughter frees.
For every bud has a tale to share,
In a concert of nature, a joyous affair.

Echoes from the Floral Path

Down the path where blossoms bounce,
Bees sing songs, and petals flounce.
"Is that a tulip prancing there?"
"Nah, just a daisy with fancy wear!"

Chirping crickets join the show,
As bumblebees declare, "We glow!"
The roses joke, with heads held high,
"Let's not forget, we're the best, oh my!"

The lilies nod, they're quite convinced,
While violets laugh, they're not dispensed.
A sunny seedling joins the fun,
"I'll be the star when day is done!"

So stroll along this flowery spree,
With chatter and chuckles, all carefree.
For in the blooms, bright and bold,
Laughter's stories forever unfold.

Sonnets of the Sunlit Path

Bright daisies dance with utmost grace,
Doing a jig in nature's place.
"Watch me shine!" a sunflower shouts,
While tiny bugs perform their bouts!

The daisies giggle, "Look at our luck,
No gardener's wrath, just nature's pluck!"
With each petal an ode to the sky,
They find humor in passing by.

"Oh dear!" says a tulip with a sigh,
"If I had legs, I'd surely fly!"
But the wind just chuckles, swaying all,
"Who needs feet when you can have a ball?"

So tread this path where smiles bloom wide,
Where flowers and fun always abide.
In every stem, in every smirk,
Sunlit sonnets, nature's perk!

Garden of Imagined Dreams

In a patch of soil, where thoughts take flight,
Grows a carrot who claims he's a knight.
He's got a crown made of leafy greens,
Defending his realm of quiet scenes!

Around him spins a merry band,
Of radishes who dance, oh so grand.
"Join us!" they cheer, "In this veggie race,
We'll turn the garden to a joyful place!"

The herbs join in, with cunning sly,
Planting jokes beneath the sky.
"Thyme to laugh!" said a sprightly sprout,
"Let's make this garden a giggly bout!"

So wander through this cheerful dream,
Where veggies frolic, and laughter's the theme.
For in this patch, both brave and sweet,
The garden of dreams is truly a treat.

Gardens of Unwritten Lines

In the plot where words do grow,
Giggling gnomes steal the show.
They waltz with weeds and dance with dirt,
While cheeky flowers wear a skirt.

Bees buzz jokes about their flight,
While sunlight shines a bit too bright.
The snapping twigs join in the fun,
As laughter echoes, everyone.

A scarecrow wears a hat askew,
Cracks puns with crows; it's quite the view.
The wind tickles petals in delight,
As butterflies join in the flight.

So come and stroll this written maze,
Where laughing blooms bring sunny rays.
In these lines, let giggles unfurl,
And share some joy with all the world.

Rhythms in the Rosebush

Roses hum a silly tune,
Swaying wildly 'neath the moon.
Thorns get tangled in the beat,
While daisies tap their little feet.

The lilies laugh on every breeze,
As bees take breaks with little teas.
In the midday sun, they pose,
Each petal wears a funny nose.

A gardener trips, the flowers squeal,
With every plant, a quirky deal.
Ode to laughter, life, and blooms,
In this jolly patch, joy looms.

So join the dance, the garden's call,
With every chuckle, we'll stand tall.
Underneath the blue, we cheer,
In rhythms strange, our hearts draw near.

Secrets of the Soil

Deep in the ground where secrets lie,
Earthworms gossip and chips do fly.
They plot and plan beneath our feet,
While rocks play games of hide and seek.

Moles wear glasses, look so wise,
With soil-stained whiskers and tiny sighs.
They share their stories, cryptic and bold,
Of the flower's dreams—so sweet, yet cold.

The roots hold hands, in tangled trust,
As beetles boast of golden rust.
Every sprinkle of rain makes them dance,
In the dark humus, they take their chance.

So dig a bit, hear the tales they share,
Of muddy miracles and garden flare.
In this earthy world where laughter swells,
Secrets abound—who knows what they tell?

Lullabies in the Lilies

Lilipads croon a bedtime song,
While frogs leap in, they don't take long.
Crickets play dream-chasing tunes,
As night falls softly, under moons.

A daisy dozes with a grin,
Swaying to dreams of chubby kin.
The breeze hums lullabies so sweet,
As stars twinkle, a cozy seat.

Everyone hushes, whispers of cheer,
As the village of blooms holds dear.
In this hush, a giggle slips,
From bumblebees with tiny tips.

So rest your head, close your eyes tight,
In the garden's arms, the world feels right.
With leafy comfort and jokes to lend,
The lilting lullabies will never end.

Verses in the Wildflower Field

I planted seeds in silly rows,
They sprouted feet and tickled toes.
The daisies danced, the tulips twirled,
In this mad parade, I laughed and whirled.

Bees in bowties buzzing near,
They're buzzing jokes—I'm all ears here!
With butterflies as my guests tonight,
We'll feast on petals under the moonlight.

A sunflower winks, what a charmer!
While the dandelions whisper, 'Be calmer!'
Their fluff holds secrets, light as air,
In this patchwork quilt, laughter we share.

The wind joins in, a jesting friend,
With chuckles that twist and twist and bend.
In this field of giggles, life feels bright,
Nature's comedy, a pure delight.

Dialogues with the Morning Dew

Morning dew drips, minty fresh,
"What's new?" I ask, feeling quite blessed.
"It's a glorious day for a splash," it glee,
"Let's dance on the grass, you and me!"

"Do you ever tire?" I curiously pry,
"Nope! I sparkle," it replied with a sigh.
"Just rolling along, giving leaves a hug,
Like a good-natured, tiny slug!"

We giggle together, just a pair,
As the day awakens, cool as fresh air.
With laughs, we sprinkle joy all around,
In each droplet, a chuckle is found.

"Stay here," I plead, "let's throw a bash!"
"I would," says dew, "but I'll melt in a flash!"
So we party in droplets, just add some flair,
And savor each moment we happily share.

Harmony of Herbaceous Hues

In the patch of green, the herbs conspire,
Basil and thyme, plotting their empire.
"Let's confuse chefs!" says cilantro bold,
"Add too much—make guacamole an uproarious mold!"

Oregano laughs, "I'm seasoning king!
Without me, what joy would your dishes bring?"
While mint, in its cool, witty air,
Says, "Stop arguing! Let's make a flair!"

Each leaf a joker, in nature's delight,
They stir up mischief from day into night.
In this herbaceous squad of green and hue,
Life's a banquet, and laughter's our brew.

Their tipsy scents waft, giggles abound,
In this garden of humor, joy's unbound.
Herbaceous companions, so merry and spry,
In every dish, oh what a joy we apply!

Inked on the Fresh Earth

With quills of grass and petals bright,
I scribble tales that take flight.
Each sprout a word, each bloom a rhyme,
Nature's own story, playful and prime.

"Did you hear that?" a worm winks sly,
"The radish wrote haikus—oh me, oh my!"
The carrots chuckle, "We're in the script!"
"More radishes!" I shout, "Let's get the trip!"

The dirt holds secrets, stories galore,
As roots entangle and spirits soar.
"What's the plot?" asks a toad, rather keen,
"Just a tale of veggies, fit for a queen!"

In this earthy canvas, laughter's the ink,
With every scribble, I pause and think.
This is the life where stories unfurl,
In the garden of whimsy, I twirl and swirl.

Hushed Secrets of the Fern Garden

In ferns that gather, whispers grow,
A dandelion tells tales, you know.
A snail in a hurry, takes his sweet time,
While beetles engage in a dance, sublime.

The starlit bees all wear tiny hats,
Debating the merits of garden chats.
A ladybug winks, with a flourish and spin,
'Who knew such gossip could fit under skin?'

The grasshoppers sing of the winds that blow,
While crickets take notes, putting on a show.
The soil, it chuckles, keeps all the score,
For who tells the best joke, gets a home on the floor.

In corners where shadows tickle the light,
A toad croaks a punchline, pure delight.
The ferns keep the secrets, but we know, my friend,
These hoots of laughter will never end.

Petal Poetry on the Weathered Stone

On stones with age, the petals lay,
Crafting limericks in a bright array.
A daisy declares, 'I'm not just a flower!'
While violets hum, taking their power.

An old butterfly, laughing in flight,
Jots down a sonnet, swirling in delight.
He stumbles and fumbles, but what a grand try,
As wind sways the buds, making them sigh.

The ants join the session, tapping their feet,
Creating a rhythm, oh what a treat!
A rock in the middle, he grumbles with glee,
'You guys are the best, I'm so glad to be free!'

As petals confide in their colorful way,
They beam under sun, brightening the day.
Nature's own poets, with humor on loan,
Scribe words of laughter, on weathered stone.

Conversations Held Behind the Hedges

Behind the hedges, secrets so sly,
A squirrel debates with a butterfly.
'Is acorn cuisine better than nectar?'
The hedgehog nods, 'Depends on the vector!'

The thorns overhear, sharpening tales,
As roses roll laughter, wagging their scales.
A vine, quite smug, raves about its twist,
While daisies shake heads, insisting, 'You missed!'

A rabbit chimes in with a laugh that erupts,
'You all are just dreamy and totally corrupt!'
The fox in the corner, sly as a fox,
Plans out a party, with snacks in the box.

So hush, little friends, as the night starts to fall,
These chatterbox plants have the best of it all.
Behind those lush hedges, where friends won't tire,
They form a cocoon of enchanting fire.

Hypnotic Waves of Honeyed Bloom

In blooms that sway, a buzzing starts,
The flowers giggle, their throaty arts.
A bee with a swagger claims all the sweets,
While sunflowers shimmer in checkered sheets.

The lilies boast of their silky touch,
A daffodil says, 'We're the best, but not much!'
Each petal spins tales of the sunlight's dance,
While tulips nod thoughtfully, caught in a trance.

Frogs croak their views on this floral spree,
Offering whispers wrapped in honeyed glee.
The air holds a chuckle, a breeze full of charm,
As butterfly whispers, 'Do you feel that alarm?'

With colors ablaze, they giggle and sway,
In the hypnotic dance of the bright sunny day.
A chorus of petals declares it's all right,
For laughter in blooms lasts far through the night.

www.ingramcontent.com/pod-product-compliance
Lightning Source LLC
Chambersburg PA
CBHW071826160426
43209CB00003B/213